How to Bake

No-Knead Bread, Rolls & Pizza

in a

Toaster Oven

From the kitchen of
Artisan Bread with Steve

Updated 5.10.2016

By
Steve Gamelin

Now that I have met the standard legal requirements I would like to give my personal exceptions. I understand this is a cookbook and anyone who purchases this book can, (a) print and share the recipes with their friends, as you do with your other cookbooks (of course, it is my hope they too will start to make no-knead bread and buy my cookbooks) and (b) you may share a recipe or two on your website, etc. as long as you note the source and provide instructions on how your audience can acquire this book.
Thanks – Steve

Table of Contents

Note from Steve

Over the years I have worked with my readers and subscribers listening to their desires and needs... to have high quality, great tasting, fresh-from-the-oven bread that is fast, convenient, hassle-free, and reliable without special equipment or expensive bakeware. In response, I developed "hands-free" technique (dough goes straight from mixing bowl to baking vessel without dusting work surface with flour or touching the dough with your hands), "roll-to-coat" (dust dough with flour in mixing bowl... no more sticky dough when shaping baguettes and rolls), and now I've added the ability to bake artisan quality bread in the toaster oven... an eco-friendly technique (consumes less energy) which is ideal for baking bread in the summer when you don't want a hot oven heating your kitchen.

This was made possible when I developed the "poor man's Dutch oven" (PMDO) which protects the crust while the crumb bakes. Simply stated, a PMDO is one bread pan covered by another bread pan. The purpose of the bottom bread pan is to shape the loaf into sandwich bread and the purpose of the cover (top bread pan) is to trap moisture from the dough in a hot, enclosed, environment. The technique emulates a Dutch oven while giving you the desired shape... sandwich bread.

These techniques are a fresh approach to bread making... I think you'll love the results.

Steve

Overview

There are three basic methods for making bread...
- **Knead by hand...** the most common method.
- **Bread machine...** very popular, but your loaf will have a silly little paddle in the bottom.
- **No-knead...** method in which Mother Nature does the kneading for you.

This cookbook uses the "no-knead" method. The advantages are...
- **No kneading...** Mother Nature does the kneading for you.
- **No yeast proofing...** instant yeast doesn't require proofing.
- **No special equipment (no mixer, no bread machine)...** entire process is done in a glass bowl with a spoon and spatula, and can be baked in a wide variety of baking vessels (bread pan, uncovered baker, skillet, preheated Dutch oven, etc.).
- **Only 4 ingredients (flour, salt, yeast and water)...** to which other ingredients can be added to make a variety of specialty breads.

There are two methods for making no-knead bread...
- **Traditional...** proofs for 8 to 24 hours.
- **"Turbo"...** ready to bake in 2-1/2 hours.

This cookbook will start by teaching you how to make no-knead bread using the traditional method, then "Turbo" method, because the traditional method is more popular and a little easier.

And we won't stop there. This cookbook will also show you how to make rolls and pizza.
- **Rolls...** you'll learn how to use bakeware to shape the rolls for you.
- **Pizza...** you'll learn how to make you own pizza dough.

What makes this cookbook different from others is...
- **"Hands-free technique"...** new and innovative technique that uses the handle end of a plastic spoon to manipulate the dough (like a dough hook) after which the dough goes straight from the mixing bowl to the baking vessel (bread pan, etc.) without dusting the work surface with flour or touching the dough with your hands.
- **"Roll-to-coat"...** innovative technique that coats the dough ball with flour in the mixing bowl. No more sticky dough. When the dough comes out of the bowl it will be easy to handle if you wish to divide the dough into portion to make baguettes, rolls, buns, long half loaves, etc.
- **"Poor man's Dutch oven"...** new and innovative technique which combines the ease of baking in a bread pan with the principles of baking in a Dutch oven.

The cookbook also includes sections that will help you understand ingredients, technique, and bakeware.

Step by step, this cookbook will take you on a journey you will love and enjoy.

Thanks - Steve

Toaster Oven vs. Conventional Oven

Cooking is very basic... take food and apply heat. The food doesn't know if it's in a conventional or toaster oven. Thus, the objective is to use appliances and bakeware that are eco-friendly and convenient without compromising the quality of food.

Advantages of the Toaster Oven
Less expensive
Eco-friendly... consumes less energy
Ideal for individual servings, small amounts and small pans
Reheats food faster and more efficiently
More efficient for toasting, warming and defrosting
Takes less time to heat up and cool down
Does not heat the entire kitchen
Uses less space
Uses a standard outlet
Can be substituted for a conventional oven or used as a second oven

Advantages of the Conventional Oven
Can do all the functions of a toaster oven and more
Ideal for large families, large amounts and large pans
Essential for popovers and other pastries
Fills the empty spot between the kitchen cabinets

Overview
Toaster ovens can do 90% of the tasks of a conventional oven consuming less energy without heating the kitchen, and newer toaster ovens have electronic temperature gages and timers which means accuracy in baking time and temperature. Toaster ovens are ideal for small kitchens, dorm rooms, in-law quarters, etc., but do not necessarily replace conventional ovens.

Two Methods for making No-Knead Dough

There are two basic methods... traditional no-knead bread and no-knead "Turbo" bread.

"Traditional" No-Knead Bread... proof for 8 to 24 hours

The traditional no-knead method uses long proofing times (8 to 24 hours) to develop flavor and was designed to be baked in a Dutch oven. The purpose of the Dutch oven is to emulate a baker's oven by trapping the moisture from the dough in a "screaming" hot, enclosed environment. This is an excellent method for making artisan quality bread.

Use: Make the dough the day before, and it will be available at your convenience any time the next day... it fits easily into your schedule.

YouTube videos in support of recipe: <u>World's Easiest No-Knead Sandwich Bread using a Poor Man's Dutch Oven</u> demonstrates traditional method.

No-Knead "Turbo" Bread... ready to bake in 1-1/2 hours

The no-knead "Turbo" method uses shorter proofing times (1-1/2 hours) and was designed to be baked in traditional bakeware (bread pan, etc.). It was designed for those who want to make no-knead bread, but... don't want to wait 8 to 24 hours. Those who want bread machine bread, but... don't want to buy and store a bread machine. It's for those of you who want a fast reliable way to make fresh-from-the-oven bread.

YouTube videos in support of recipe: <u>How to Bake No-Knead Bread in a Toaster Oven (no mixer... no bread machine... "hands-free" technique)</u> demonstrates "Turbo" method.

Use: No need to plan ahead... your dough will be ready to bake in less than 2-1/2 hours.

Taste Comparison

In our taste tests... no one could tell the difference in taste, texture, crust or crumb between the two methods.

"Turbo" Ingredients & Technique

To make no-knead "Turbo" bread (vs. traditional) there are two changes... ingredients and sound proofing technique.

One - Ingredients

Yeast is the active ingredient that makes the dough rise, thus shorter proofing times require more yeast (1-1/4 vs. 1/4 tsp yeast).

Two - Sound proofing technique

Shorter proofing times require a warm bowl, warm ingredients and warm proofing environment. The ideal temperature for proofing is 78 to 85 degrees F, but the typically home is 68 to 72 degrees, which is why recipes generally suggest proofing in a "warm draft-free environment". So, you have a choice... wait longer for the dough to proof or create a warm proofing environment. My favorite techniques for creating a warm proofing environment are...

Oven setting: If your oven has a setting for proofing (80 degrees F)... use it.

Direct sunlight: Cover bowl with plastic wrap, place in direct sunlight, and the heat from the Sun will create a more favorable proofing environment.

Oven light: If your oven has a light... cover bowl with plastic wrap, place in oven, turn light on, and close the door. The oven light will generate heat and increase the temperature inside the oven by several degrees. The amount of heat will depend on the size of the oven and strength of the bulb. The oven temperature will start low and climb slowly. Each oven is different, so check periodically until you are familiar with the nature of your oven.

This is my personal favorite. The result is consistent... sunny or cloudy... summer or winter.

Desk Lamp: Cover bowl with plastic wrap, place under a desk lamp, lower lamp so that it's close to the bowl, and turn lamp on. The plastic wrap over the bowl will create a similar effect to leaving car windows rolled up on a sunny day.

Supporting video: How to Proof Bread Dough (a.k.a. The Dynamics of Proofing)

Guide to "Poor Man's Dutch Oven" (PMDO)

The problem with baking bread in a toaster oven using conventional bakeware is... the crust over bakes before the crumb is baked. Solution... use a "poor man's Dutch oven" (PMDO). A PMDO protects the crust while the crumb bakes.

Simply stated, a "poor man's Dutch oven" (PMDO) is one bread pan covered by another bread pan. The purpose of the bottom bread pan is to shape the loaf into sandwich bread and the purpose of the cover (top bread pan) is to trap the moisture from the dough in a hot, enclosed, environment. The technique emulates a Dutch oven while giving you the desired shape (sandwich bread).

The concept of using a "poor man's Dutch oven" to bake sandwich bread is a new technique, thus I felt it was important to test the options. While testing bread pans I didn't learn anything earth-shaking, but I did learn some good general rules.

Sizes: There are four basic sizes... small (8" x 4") for small loaves like raisin bread, medium (8-1/2" x 4-1/2") and large (9" x 5") for standard loaves, and long (12" x 4-1/2") for long and half loaves.

The four PMDOs in the picture from left to right are...
- Good Cook premium nonstick loaf pan (8" x 4" x 2-1/4") (Liquid capacity: 42 oz)... excellent for raisin bread and other small (3 cups flour) loaves.
- OXO Good Gripe Non-Stick Pro 1 lb Loaf Pan (8-1/2" x 4-1/2" x 2-4/5") (Liquid capacity: 52 oz)... my personnel favorite.
- Good Cook premium nonstick loaf pan (9" x 5" x 2-1/4") (Liquid capacity: 64 oz)... excellent and inexpensive.
- Wilton long loaf pan (12" x 4-1/2" x 3-1/8") (Liquid capacity: 76 oz)... ideal for long and half loaves (get 4 if you wish to make half loaves).

Liquid capacity is import, because some bread pans are not properly marked.

Shape: You can use either a 9" x 5" or 8-1/2" x 4-1/2" bread pan for a 1 pound loaf (3-1/2 cups flour) but the shape will be a little different. The 9" x 5" bread pan will give you a little wider loaf and the 8-1/2" x 4-1/2" bread pan will give you a little taller loaf.

I like pans with flat rims, thin handles and round corners. Flat rims... fit together better and are more stable. Thin handles... allows me to use binder clips. Round corners... are easier to clean.

Fasteners: You really don't need to fasten the top pan to the bottom, but it's more secure and stable. My favorite fastener is the standard binder clip which is available in the office supply section of many stores. I use both medium and large binder clips depending on the shape of the bread pan's handles.

Type: Metal pans were the clear winner. They heat faster and did an excellent job baking the crumb and developing the crust. Loaf pans made of glass and cast iron did not fare as well. The internal temperature was 200+ degrees F (just like the others), but the crust did not develop as well and the top had a tendency to sag.

YouTube videos in support of recipes: <u>World's Easiest No-Knead Sandwich Bread using a Poor Man's Dutch Oven</u> demonstrates traditional method and <u>How to Bake No-Knead Bread in a Toaster Oven (no mixer... no bread machine... "hands-free" technique)</u> demonstrates "Turbo" method.

Ingredients

It only takes four ingredients to make bread... flour, salt, yeast and water.

Flour

Flour is the base ingredient of bread and there are four basic types of flour...

(1) Bread flour is designed for yeast bread. It has a higher percentage of gluten which gives artisan bread its airy crumb.

(2) All-purpose flour has less gluten than bread flour. I use all-purpose flour for biscuits, flatbreads, etc. In other words... I use it when I don't want an airy crumb.

(3) Self-rising flour is all-purpose flour with baking soda and baking powder added as leavening agents. It's intended for quick breads... premixed and ready to go. Do not use self-rising flour to make yeast bread. To see the difference between yeast and quick breads you may want to watch Introduction to No-Knead Beer Bread (a.k.a. Artisan Yeast Beer Bread) and Introduction to Quick Beer Bread (a.k.a. Beer Bread Dinner Rolls).

(4) And there are a variety of specialty flours... whole wheat, rye, and a host of others. Each has its unique flavor and characteristics. In some cases, you can substitute specialty flour for bread flour, but you may need to tweak the recipe because most specialty flours have less gluten. I frequently blend specialty flour with bread flour.

8

Flour is the primary ingredient... if you don't use the correct flour you won't get the desired results.

Note: To know how many cups of flour there are in a specific bag... it's typically on the side in "Nutritional Facts". For example, this bag reads, "Serving Size 1/4 cup... Serving Per Container about 75". In other words... 18.75 (75 times 1/4). That's the technical answer, but in the real world (measuring cup versus weight) a bag of flour will measure differently based on density (sifted versus unsifted), type of flour (wheat is more dense than bread flour), humidity (flour weighs more on humid days), and all the other variables life and nature have to offer. Thus, there is no single correct answer, but for practical purposes... figure a 5 lb bag of bread flour is 17 to 18 cups.

Salt
While it is possible to make bread without salt... you would be disappointed. There are three basics types of salt...

(1) Most baking recipes are designed to use everyday table salt unless specified otherwise. Unless you're experienced, it is probably smartest to use table salt for your baking needs.

(2) Kosher salt is excellent. I use it when I cook, but a tablespoon of kosher salt does not equal a tablespoon of table salt because kosher salt crystals are larger.

(3) And, I use specialty salt as a garnish... for appearance and taste. For example, I use sea salt to garnish pretzels.

Generally speaking, when salt is added as an ingredient and baked it is difficult to taste the difference between table, kosher and sea salt. When salt is added as a garnish and comes in contact with the taste buds... kosher or specialty salt is an excellent choice.

Yeast
Yeast is the "magic" ingredient which transforms flour and water into dough. My traditional no-knead recipes use 1/4 tsp yeast... I want the dough to rise slowly which allows the dough to develop flavor. My "Turbo" recipes use 1-1/4 tsp yeast... I want a faster rises like traditional bread recipes. There are three basic types of yeast...

(1) The most common is active dry yeast which needs to be proof in warm water prior to being added to flour.

(2) I use instant dry yeast (a.k.a. "instant yeast", "bread machine yeast", "quick rise", "rapid rise", "fast rising", etc.) which does not need to be proofed in warm water. It is a more recent development which is more

potent and reliable... and why worry about proofing yeast if you don't have too.

(3) Some older recipes call for <u>cake yeast</u> (a.k.a. "compressed yeast" or "fresh yeast"), but it's perishable. Most bakers substitute active and instant dry yeast for cake yeast when using older recipes.

The names on the bottles can be confusing. When in doubt, read the instructions and look for one that does not require soaking the yeast in warm water prior to use.

Water

Water hydrates the ingredients and activates the yeast. The no-knead method uses a little more water than the typical recipe... and that's a good thing. It makes it easier to combine the wet and dry ingredients, and contributes to its airy crumb.

(1) I use <u>tap water</u>. It's convenient and easy, but sometimes city water has too much chlorine (chlorine kills yeast).

(2) If your dough does not rise during first proofing you may want to use <u>bottled drinking water</u>.

(3) But, do not use <u>distilled water</u> because the minerals have been removed.

Water is a flavor ingredient, if your water doesn't taste good... use bottled drinking water.

Flavor Ingredients

It only takes four ingredients to make bread... flour, salt, yeast and water, to which a variety of flavor ingredients can be added to make specialty breads such as... honey whole wheat, multi-grain white, rosemary, Mediterranean olive, cinnamon raisin, honey oatmeal, and a host of others.

Technique & Tips

The techniques used to make traditional and "Turbo" no-knead bread are identical except proofing. Turbo uses shorter proofing times, thus it is important to use sound proofing technique (a warm proofing environment) when using the "Turbo" method. The traditional method is demonstrated on YouTube in World's Easiest No-Knead Sandwich Bread using a Poor Man's Dutch Oven (using a conventional oven) and the "Turbo" method is demonstrated in How to Bake No-Knead Bread in a Toaster Oven (no mixer... no bread machine... "hands-free" technique).

Prep
Traditional: Because the traditional method proof for 8 to 24 hours it uses cool water to slow the proofing process, thus the temperature of the bowl is not important.

Turbo: To insure consistency and assist Mother Nature with proofing... it's important to provide yeast with a warm proofing environment. One of the keys to proofing temperature is the temperature of the mixing bowl because it has direct contact with the dough. Thus, use a bowl that is warm to the touch so that the bowl doesn't draw the heat out of the warm water.

Combining Ingredients
Pour water in a 3 to 4 qt glass mixing bowl (use warm water and a warm bowl for "Turbo" and cool for traditional). Add salt, yeast, flavor ingredients, etc... and stir to combine (it will insure the ingredients are evenly distributed). Add flour (flour will resist the water and float). Start by stirring the ingredients with the handle end of a plastic spoon drawing the flour from the sides into the middle of bowl (vigorously mixing will not hydrate the flour faster... but it will raise a lot of dust). Within 30 seconds the flour will hydrate and form a shaggy ball. Then scrape dry flour from side of bowl and tumble dough to combine moist flour with dry flour (about 15 seconds). It takes about one minute to combine wet and dry ingredients.

Traditional: Cover bowl with plastic wrap, place on counter, and proof for 8 to 24 hours.

Turbo: Cover bowl with plastic wrap, place in a warm draft free location, and proof for 1-1/2 hours.

1st Proofing (bulk fermentation)
The process is called "proofing" because it "proves" the yeast is active.

Bread making is nature at work (yeast is a living organism) and subject to nature. Seasons (summer vs. winter) and weather (heat & humidity) have a direct impact on proofing. In other words, don't worry if your dough varies in size... that's Mother Nature. Just focus on your goal... if the gluten forms (dough develops a stringy nature) and doubles in size... you're good to go.

If your dough does <u>not</u> rise the usual culprits are... outdated yeast or chlorinated water (chlorine kills yeast). Solution, get fresh yeast and/or use bottled drinking water.

If your dough is <u>slow</u> (takes "forever") to rise... your proofing temperature is probably too cool.

Traditional: Because the traditional method use long proofing times (8 to 24 hours) it does not require any special technique.

Turbo: Because "Turbo" dough use shorter proofing times (1-12/ hours) it is important to practice sound proofing technique.

The ideal temperature for proofing is 78 to 85 degrees F, but the typically home is 68 to 72 degrees, which is why recipes generally suggest proofing in a "warm draft-free environment". So, you have a choice... wait longer or create a warm proofing environment. My favorites are...

Oven setting: If your oven has a setting for proofing (80 degrees F)... use it.

Direct sunlight: Cover bowl with plastic wrap, place in direct sunlight, and the heat from the Sun will create a favorable proofing environment.

Oven light: If your oven has a light... cover bowl with plastic wrap, place in oven, turn light on, and close the door. The oven light will generate heat and increase the temperature inside the oven by several degrees. The amount of heat will depend on the size of the oven and strength of the bulb. The oven temperature will always start low and climb slowly, but it may go over 90 degrees F. so check periodically until you are familiar with the nature of your oven.

Desk Lamp: Cover bowl with plastic wrap, place under a desk lamp, lower lamp so that it's close to the bowl, and turn lamp on. The plastic wrap over the bowl will create a similar effect to leaving car windows rolled up on a sunny day.

Microwave: Place an 8 to 16 oz cup of water in the microwave and heat on high for 2 minutes. Then move the cup to the back corner, place mixing bowl (dough) in microwave and close the door. The heat and steam from the hot water will create a favorable environment for proofing.

Folding dough proofer: Commercial bakeries have large proofing ovens in which they can control climate and temperature. There are smaller versions available for the public that fold flat.

Tip: To fit bread making into your schedule... you can extend 1st proofing up to 4 hours (or even more), but don't shorten... it important to give Mother Nature time to form the gluten.

Degas, Pull & Stretch

The purpose of degassing, pulling and stretching is to, (a) expel the gases that formed during bulk fermentation, (b) strengthen the dough by realigning and stretching the gluten strands, and (c) stimulate yeast activity for 2nd proofing.

Because no-knead dough is sticky and difficult to handle... I degas, pull & stretch dough by stirring it in the bowl with the handle end of a plastic spoon (like a dough hook). It will reduce the size of the dough ball by 50% making it easier to handle and the process replaces folding and shaping in most cases.

Roll-to-Coat

Before removing the dough from bowl... dust the dough and side of the bowl with flour, then roll-to-coat. The flour will bond to the sticky dough making it easier to handle, but do not roll-to-coat with flour if you're going to garnish or baste.

Garnish & Baste

The purpose of garnishing and basting is to enhance the appearance of the crust, but it isn't necessary. If you decide to garnish and baste there are two techniques... roll-to-coat and skillet method.

Roll-to-Coat Method: Before removing dough from bowl... add ingredients to bowl (on the dough and side of the bowl), then roll to coat. For example, when I garnish honey oatmeal bread... I sprinkle oat in the bowl and on the dough, then roll the dough ball in the oats and they will bond to the sticky dough. This can also be done with seeds, grains, olive oil, egg wash, etc.

Skillet Method: When I want to garnish and/or baste the top of the loaf... I coat the proofing skillet with baste (egg wash, olive oil, vegetable oil, etc.) and sprinkle with the garnish (oats, seeds, grains, etc.). The ingredients will bond with the dough as the dough proofs.

Supporting video: <u>How to Garnish & Baste No-Knead Bread using "Hands-Free" Technique</u>

Divide & Shape

If you're not going to divide the dough... it can go straight from the mixing bowl to the proofing skillet or baking vessel. If you are going to divide and shape the dough... dust the dough and side of the bowl with flour and roll-to-coat, dust work surface with flour, roll the dough ball out of the bowl (excess flour and all) onto the work surface, and divide and shape. I use a plastic bowl scraper to assist in dividing, shaping and carry the dough to the baking vessel. Together they (flour & bowl scraper) make it easier to handle the dough.

2nd Proofing
Traditional: Originally I proofed for 1 to 2 hours, but over time I have been baking more in bread pans and found shorter proofing times gave better results. I now proof for 30 to 60 minutes.

Turbo: Place dough in a warm draft-free location and proof for 30 minutes.

Tip: To fit bread making into your schedule... you can extend 2nd proofing times, but you don't want the dough to exceed the size of the baking vessel. If you're using a large baking vessel (Dutch oven, etc.) it's never a problem, but if you're using a bread pan don't allow the dough to exceed the sides of the pan before baking or your loaf will droop over the sides and be less attractive. But, always bake it... it will still be delicious.

Score
The purpose of scoring dough is to provide seams to control where the crust will split during "oven spring", but it isn't necessary to score dough. If you do decide to score your loaf you may want to use a scissors (no-knead dough is very moist and more likely to stretch than slice). Personally, I place the dough in the baking vessel seam side up... the dough will split at the seam during "oven spring" which gives the loaf a nice rustic appearance.

Bake
Baking Time: Bread is done when it reaches an internal temperature of 185 to 220 degrees F. and the crumb (inside of the bread) isn't doughy. Baking times in my recipes are designed to give bread an internal temperature of 200 to 205 degrees F, but ovens vary and you may need to adjust your baking times slightly.

No-Stick Spray: Most bakeware has a non-stick surface, but it is safest to spray your bakeware unless you are fully confident your bread won't stick.

Ovens: Ovens aren't always accurate. I check the temperature of ovens and bakeware. Ovens with a digital readout that displays the temperature as they preheat are typically very accurate, but ovens that say they will be at temperature in a specific number of minutes are not always accurate. My point is... you will get the best results if you learn the character and nature of your oven.

Oven Rack: Generally speaking you want to bake bread and rolls in the middle or lower third of the oven, but it isn't critical. Just keep them away from the upper heating element or they may brown a little too quickly.

Oven Spring: When dough is first put into the oven it will increase in size by as much as a third in a matter of minutes because, (a) gases trapped in the dough will expand, (b) moisture will turn into steam and try to push its way out, and (c) yeast will become highly active converting sugars into gases. The steam and gases work together to create "oven spring". Once the internal temperature of the bread reaches 120 degrees F... the yeast will begin to die and the crust will harden.

Storing Bread & Dough
After allowing bread to cool... it can be wrapped in plastic wrap, or stored in a zip-lock plastic bag, or plastic bread bags (available on the web). If you wish to keep bread for a longer period of time... slice it into portions and freeze them in a zip-lock freezer bag (remove excess air). Do not store bread in the refrigerator. Bread goes stale faster in the refrigerator.

If you wish to save dough... divide it into portions, drizzle each portion with olive oil, place in zip-lock bag, remove excess air, and refrigerate for up to two days or freeze for up to two months. To thaw dough... move dough from freezer to refrigerator the day before (12 or more hours), then place on counter for 30 minutes before use to come to room temperature.

Equipment & Bakeware
Bowl for Mixing: You can use any 3 to 4 qt bowl. I use a 3-1/2 qt glass bowl because, (a) there's ample room for the dough to expand, (b) plastic wrap sticks to glass, and (c) I don't want the rim of my bowl to exceed the width of the plastic wrap.

Measuring Spoons: I'm sure you already have measuring spoons in the kitchen... they will work just fine. If you're going to buy new, I prefer oval versus round because an oval shape will fit into jars and containers more easily.

Measuring Cups: Dry measuring cups are designed to be filled to the top and leveled. Liquid measuring cups have a pour spout and are designed to be filled to the gradations on the side (neither measures weight). Because of their design and a slight difference in volume, it is best to use the appropriate measuring cup.

Note: U.S. and metric measuring cups may be used interchangeably... there is only a slight difference (±3%). More importantly, the ingredients of a recipe measured with a set (U.S. or metric) will have their volumes in the same proportion to one another.

Spoon for Combining Wet and Dry Ingredients: A spoon is an excellent tool for combining wet and dry ingredients. Surprisingly, I found the handle end of a plastic spoon worked best for me because, I didn't have a big clump on the end like some of my other mixing utensils (which makes it easier to stir and manipulate the dough). And when you think about it... mixers don't use a paddle to mix dough, they use a hook which looks a lot like the handle end of my spoon.

Silicon Baking Mat: Silicone baking mats are very useful... I use them as reusable parchment paper (they're environmentally friendly). Silicone baking mats serve two purposes... (a) as a work surface for folding and shaping (they have excellent non-stick properties), and (b) as a baking mat... specifically when the dough is difficult to move after folding and shaping. And I slide a cookie sheet under the mat before baking (it makes it easier to put the mat into and take it out of the oven).

Spatula: I use a spatula to scrape the sides of the bowl to get the last bits of flour incorporated into the dough.

Plastic Bowl Scraper: I use a plastic bowl scraper verses a metal dough scraper because it's the better multi-tasker. I use the bowl scraper to (a) fold, shape, and divide the dough, (b) assist in transporting the dough to the proofing vessel, (c) scrape excess flour off the work surface, (d) scrape excess flour out of the bowl (after all it is a bowl scraper), and (e) scrape any remaining bits in the sink towards the disposal. It's a useful multi-tasker and you can't do all those tasks with a metal cough scraper.

Timer: I'm sure you already have a timer and it will work just fine. If you're thinking about a new one... I prefer digital because they're more accurate.

Proofing Baskets & Vessels: The purpose of a proofing basket or vessel is to pre-shape the dough prior to baking (dough will spread if it isn't contained). Because no-knead dough has a tendency to stick to the lining of proofing baskets... I use common household items as proofing vessels. For example, I use an 8" skillet (with no-stick spray) to pre-shape dough when baking in a Dutch oven. It shapes the dough during proofing, and the handle makes it easy to carry the dough and put it in the hot Dutch oven safely.

You can also proof dough in the baking vessel if it doesn't have to be preheated. For example, standard loaves are typically proof and baked in the bread pan where your bread pan shapes the loaf during proofing and baking. You can use this same principle for shaping and baking rolls and buns.

Baking Vessels: Baking vessels come in a variety of sizes, shapes and materials. You can change the appearance of the loaf by sampling changing the baking vessel.

Plastic Wrap & Proofing Towel: I use plastic wrap for 1st proofing and a lint-free towel for 2nd proofing. Plastic wrap protects dough for longer proofing times and can be used to create a favorable proofing environment (solar effect).

Cooling Rack: The purpose of a cooling rack is to expose the bottom of the loaf during the cooling process.

Bread Bags: I use plastic bread bags to store bread after they have cooled. And they're great for packaging bread as gifts. I also use paper bags as gifts when the loaf is still warm and I don't want to trap the moisture in a plastic bag... it gives a nice natural appearance.

10" Flat Whisk: I use a flat whisk to combine dry ingredients with yogurt... a flat whisk will slice through yogurt forming small clump. If you use a balloon whisk a big lump will form inside the balloon.

Pastry/Pizza Roller: When you watch shows they hand shape and toss pizza dough, but I find it more practical to use a pastry/pizza roller. It is also useful when shaping flatbread and cinnamon rolls.

"I know when food is supposed to be served in a bowl with a name on it."
Fran Fine - "The Nanny"

No-Knead Bread & Rolls Baked in a Toaster Oven

No-knead bread can be baked in a toaster oven. The key is to protect the crust from the upper heating element. My solution is simple... I use a poor man's Dutch oven. Simply stated, a "poor man's Dutch oven" (PMDO) is a bread pan covered by another bread pan. The purpose of the bottom bread pan is to shape the loaf into sandwich bread and the purpose of the cover (top bread pan) is to trap the moisture from the dough in a hot, enclosed environment. In other words... I replaced the standard Dutch oven with two bread pan to get the desired shape... sandwich bread, and protected the crust from the upper heating element.

Baking bread, rolls and pizza in a toaster oven is ideal for those with limited kitchens and those of you who don't want to turn the oven on because it heats the house in the summer.

This cookbook will focus on baking in a toaster oven while giving the option of baking in a conventional oven. The process for making the dough is the same, but the baking time and temperature is different.

YouTube videos in support of recipe: World's Easiest No-Knead Sandwich Bread using a Poor Man's Dutch Oven demonstrates traditional method and How to Bake No-Knead Bread in a Toaster Oven (no mixer... no bread machine... "hands-free" technique) demonstrates "Turbo" method.

Country White Bread (PMDO | traditional method)
Country white is the most popular bread. It's simple... it's basic. And, if you're making your first loaf... this is the place to start.

Picture: For lunch I made an egg salad sandwich... a little lettuce and my special egg salad between a couple slices of fresh-from-the-oven country white bread. To make my special egg salad I use... 12 hard boiled eggs (sliced with a egg slicer and cut down the middle), 4 heaping tbsp mayo, 1 heaping tbsp yellow mustard, 1 heaping tbsp sweet pickle relish and a tsp salt.

Options:
"Turbo" method: If you wish to reduce the proofing time from 8 hours to 1-1/2 hours... increase yeast from 1/4 to 1-1/4 tsp and proof in a warm draft free environment (78 to 85 degrees F).
Conventional oven: Preheat oven to 400 degrees F. and bake for 40 minutes with the top on and 3 to 15 minutes with the top off to finish the crust.

Country White Bread

Pour water into a 3 to 4 qt glass mixing bowl.

> 14 oz cool Water

Add salt and yeast... give a quick stir to combine.

> 1-1/2 tsp Salt
>
> 1/4 tsp Instant Yeast

Add flour... stir until dough forms a shaggy ball, scrape dry flour from side of bowl, then tumble dough to combine moist flour with dry flour.

> 3-1/2 cups Bread Flour

Cover bowl with plastic wrap, place on counter, and proof for 8 to 24 hours.

8 to 24 hours later (PMDO | toaster oven)

When dough has risen and developed its gluten structure... spray bottom bread pan (8-1/2" x 4-1/2" or 9" x 5") with no-stick cooking spray and set aside.

"Degas, pull and stretch"... stick handle end of a plastic spoon in the dough and stir (dough will form a sticky ball). Then, scrape side of bowl to get remainder of the dough into the sticky dough ball.

Roll dough out of bowl into bread pan.

Cover bottom pan with top pan, secure with binder clips, and place PMDO in a warm draft-free location to proof for 30 minutes.

30 minutes later

Place PMDO in toaster oven, set oven to 400 degrees F, and bake for 45 minutes with the top on and 3 to 10 with the top off to finish the crust.

45 to 55 minutes later

Remove pan from oven, gently turn loaf out on work surface and place on cooling rack.

Italian Sesame Bread (PMDO | "Turbo" method)
Here's a bread everyone is sure to enjoy and it's remarkable easy to garnish no-knead bread using the "hands-free" & "roll-to-coat" technique. I used two 8-1/2" x 4-1/2" OXO bread pans, but 9" x 5" pans are perfectly acceptable.

Note:
When proofing for 1-1/2 hours vs. 8 to 24 hours... it's important to proof in a warm draft-free environment. The ideal proofing temperature is 78 to 85 degrees F, but most of our homes are 68 to 73 degrees. So... to create a favorable proofing environment I place the bowl under my desk lamp where the plastic wrap on the bowl traps the heat and raise the temperature inside the bowl to a little over 80 degrees (solar affect).

Options:
Add sesame and flax seed: You can create an interesting appearance, texture and flavor by adding 1 Tbsp (each) sesame and flax seeds to the dough.
"Traditional" method: If you wish to proof overnight using the traditional method... decrease yeast from 1-1/4 tsp to 1/4 tsp and proof 8 to 24 hours.
Conventional oven: Preheat oven to 400 degrees F. and bake for 40 minutes with the top on and 3 to 15 minutes with the top off to finish the crust.

YouTube Video in support of recipe: No-Knead Bread 101 (Includes demonstration of Sesame Seed Bread... Italian, Muffuletta, & Sandwich)

Italian Sesame Bread

Pour warm water in a 3 to 4 qt warm glass mixing bowl (use a warm bowl... you don't want a cold bowl to take the heat out of the warm water).

> 14 oz warm Water

Add salt, yeast and olive oil... give a quick stir to combine.

> 1-1/2 tsp Salt
> 1-1/4 tsp Instant Yeast
> 1 Tbsp Extra Virgin Olive Oil
> 1 Tbsp Sesame Seeds (optional)
> 1 Tbsp Flax Seeds (optional)

Add flour... stir until dough forms a shaggy ball, scrape dry flour from side of bowl, then tumble dough to combine moist flour with dry flour.

> 3-1/2 cups Bread Flour

Cover bowl with plastic wrap, place in a warm draft-free location, and proof for 1-1/2 hours.

1-1/2 hours later (PMDO | garnish| toaster oven)

When dough has risen and developed its gluten structure... spray bottom bread pan (8-1/2" x 4-1/2" or 9" x 5") with no-stick cooking spray and set aside.

"Degas, pull and stretch"... stick handle end of a plastic spoon in the dough and stir (dough will form a sticky ball). Then, scrape side of bowl to get remainder of the dough into the sticky dough ball.

Garnish... sprinkle dough ball and side of bowl with sesame seeds, and roll-to-coat (roll dough ball in seeds to coat).

> 2 Tbsp Sesame Seeds

Roll dough out of bowl into bread pan.

Cover bottom pan with top pan, secure with binder clips, and place PMDO in a warm draft-free location to proof for 30 minutes.

30 minutes later

Place PMDO in toaster oven, set oven to 400 degrees F, and bake for 45 minutes with the top on and 3 to 10 with the top off to finish the crust.

45 to 55 minutes later

Remove pan from oven, gently turn loaf out on work surface and place on cooling rack.

Cheddar Cheese Bread (PMDO)

Fresh-from-the-oven bread is special... add cheese and you have a winner. Something your friends and guests will love. This is a remarkably simple recipe that everyone is sure to enjoy.

Picture: For lunch I made a cheese sandwich. I spread mayo and yellow mustard on two slices fresh-from-the-oven cheddar cheese bread, added two slices of cheddar, two slices Swiss, one slice provolone cheese.

Options:

<u>"Turbo" method</u>: If you wish to reduce the proofing time from 8 hours to 1-1/2 hours... increase yeast from 1/4 to 1-1/4 tsp and proof in a warm draft free environment (78 to 85 degrees F).

<u>Conventional oven</u>: Preheat oven to 400 degrees F. and bake for 40 minutes with the top on and 3 to 15 minutes with the top off to finish the crust.

Cheddar Cheese Bread

Pour water into a 3 to 4 qt glass mixing bowl.

> 16 oz cool Water

Add salt and yeast... give a quick stir to combine.

> 1-1/2 tsp Salt
> 1/4 tsp Instant Yeast

Add flour... then cheese (if cheese is added before flour it will be harder to combine)... stir until dough forms a shaggy ball, scrape dry flour from side of bowl, then tumble dough to combine moist flour with dry flour.

> 3-1/2 cups Bread Flour
> 1 cup coarsely shredded Cheddar Cheese

Cover bowl with plastic wrap, place on counter, and proof for 8 to 24 hours.

8 to 24 hours later (PMDO | toaster oven)

When dough has risen and developed its gluten structure... spray bread pan (8-1/2" x 4-1/2" or 9" x 5") with no-stick cooking spray and set aside.

"Degas, pull and stretch"... stick handle end of a plastic spoon in the dough and stir (dough will form a sticky ball). Then, scrape side of bowl to get remainder of the dough into the sticky dough ball.

Roll dough out of bowl into bread pan.

Cover bottom pan with top pan, secure with binder clips, and place PMDO in a warm draft-free location to proof for 30 minutes.

30 minutes later

Place PMDO in toaster oven, set oven to 400 degrees F, and bake for 45 minutes with the top on and 3 to 10 with the top off to finish the crust.

45 to 55 minutes later

Remove pan from oven, gently turn loaf out on work surface and place on cooling rack.

Multigrain Country White Bread (PMDO)

If you haven't made multigrain bread before, this is an excellent choice for your first loaf. Simple recipe... simple flavors... universally pleasing taste. In fact, it's one of my most popular loaves. My first multigrain loaves used 2 cups bread flour and 1 cup wheat flour. One time I forgot the wheat flour and used 3 cups bread flour. Surprise, surprise, surprise... the multigrain country white became one of my most popular breads. I had assumed those who liked grains also liked wheat breads, but there appears to be a significant segment of our society who likes multigrain bread without the wheat bread taste. Wheat is one of those things you either like or don't like, but it doesn't mean you don't like multigrain bread.

Picture: For lunch I made a tuna salad sandwich... a little lettuce cupped to hold the tuna salad between a couple slices of fresh-from-the-oven multigrain country white bread. My tuna salad is made of... 1 can (12 oz) chunk light tuna in oil (drain the oil), 2 heaping tbsp mayo, 2 heaping tsp sweet pickle relish and 1 heaping tsp yellow mustard.

Options:
"Turbo" method: If you wish to reduce the proofing time from 8 hours to 1-1/2 hours... increase yeast from 1/4 to 1-1/4 tsp and proof in a warm draft free environment (78 to 85 degrees F).
Conventional oven: Preheat oven to 400 degrees F. and bake for 40 minutes with the top on and 3 to 15 minutes with the top off to finish the crust.

Multigrain Country White Bread

Pour water into a 3 to 4 qt glass mixing bowl.

    16 oz cool Water

Add salt, yeast and seeds... give a quick stir to combine.

    1-1/2 tsp Salt
    1/4 tsp Instant Yeast
    1 Tbsp Sesame Seeds
    1 Tbsp Flax Seeds

Add flour... then oats (if oats are added before flour they will absorb the water and it will be harder to combine)... stir until dough forms a shaggy ball, scrape dry flour from side of bowl, then tumble dough to combine moist flour with dry flour.

    3-1/2 cups Bread Flour
    1/2 cup Old Fashioned Quaker Oats

Cover bowl with plastic wrap, place on counter, and proof for 8 to 24 hours.

8 to 24 hours later (PMDO| toaster oven)

When dough has risen and developed its gluten structure... spray bread pan (8-1/2" x 4-1/2" or 9" x 5") with no-stick cooking spray and set aside.

"Degas, pull and stretch"... stick handle end of a plastic spoon in the dough and stir (dough will form a sticky ball). Then, scrape side of bowl to get remainder of the dough into the sticky dough ball.

Roll dough out of bowl into bread pan.

Cover bottom pan with top pan, secure with binder clips, and place PMDO in a warm draft-free location to proof for 30 minutes.

30 minutes later

Place PMDO in toaster oven, set oven to 400 degrees F, and bake for 45 minutes with the top on and 3 to 10 with the top off to finish the crust.

45 to 55 minutes later

Remove pan from oven, gently turn loaf out on work surface and place on cooling rack.

Beer Bread (small PMDO)

There are two basic types of beer bread... yeast and quick. Yeast beer bread uses yeast as a leavening agent. Quick beer bread uses self rising flour which has baking soda and baking powder as leavening agents. Quick beer bread is—as the name implies—very quick and easy, but don't let that fool you. It makes delicious rolls. To see the difference between yeast and quick you may want to watch, Introduction to No-Knead Beer Bread (a.k.a. Artisan Yeast Beer Bread) and Introduction to Quick Beer Bread (a.k.a. Beer Bread Dinner Rolls). I used two undersized *Wilton* 8-1/2" x 4-1/2" bread pans for my PMDO.

Picture: For lunch I made a stadium bratwurst & bacon sandwich. I spread mayo and yellow mustard on two slices fresh-from-the-oven beer bread, sliced the bratwursts in half (1-1/2 brats per sandwich), topped it with a slice of bacon and, of course, I had it with beer.

Options:
Larger loaf: Use 3-1/2 vs. 3 cups flour, increase beer (or water) by 2 oz and increase baking time with the top on by 5 minutes.
"Turbo" method: If you wish to reduce the proofing time from 8 hours to 1-1/2 hours... increase yeast from 1/4 to 1-1/4 tsp and proof in a warm draft free environment (78 to 85 degrees F).
Conventional oven: Preheat oven to 400 degrees F. and bake for 35 minutes with the top on and 3 to 15 minutes with the top off to finish the crust.

Beer Bread

Pour room temperature beer into a 3 to 4 qt glass mixing bowl.

> 12 oz room temperature Beer

Add yeast... give a quick stir to combine.

> 1/4 tsp Instant Yeast

Add salt (salt will foam)... give a quick stir to combine.

> 1-1/2 tsp Salt

Add flour... stir until dough forms a shaggy ball, scrape dry flour from side of bowl, then tumble dough to combine moist flour with dry flour.

> 3 cups Bread Flour

Cover bowl with plastic wrap, place on counter, and proof for 8 to 24 hours.

8 to 24 hours later (small PMDO | toaster oven)

When dough has risen and developed its gluten structure... spray bread pan (8" x 4" or under sized 8-1/2" x 4-1/2") with no-stick cooking spray and set aside.

"Degas, pull and stretch"... stick handle end of a plastic spoon in the dough and stir (dough will form a sticky ball). Then, scrape side of bowl to get remainder of the dough into the sticky dough ball.

Roll dough out of bowl into bread pan.

Cover bottom pan with top pan, secure with binder clips, and place PMDO in a warm draft-free location to proof for 30 minutes.

30 minutes later

Place PMDO in toaster oven, set oven to 400 degrees F, and bake for 40 minutes with the top on and 3 to 10 with the top off to finish the crust.

40 to 50 minutes later

Remove pan from oven, gently turn loaf out on work surface and place on cooling rack.

Honey Oatmeal Bread (PMDO)

Fresh-from-the-oven bread with the wholesome goodness of oats and the sweetness of honey... what's not to like? This loaf is as delicious to eat as it is pleasing to the eye.

Picture: For lunch I made a country fried steak sandwich... I spread mayo on two slices fresh-from-the-oven honey oatmeal bread with lettuce, tomato and a precooked country fried steak that I heated in the toaster oven. Simple and delicious.

Options:
"Turbo" method: If you wish to reduce the proofing time from 8 hours to 1-1/2 hours... increase yeast from 1/4 to 1-1/4 tsp and proof in a warm draft free environment (78 to 85 degrees F).
Conventional oven: Preheat oven to 400 degrees F. and bake for 40 minutes with the top on and 3 to 15 minutes with the top off to finish the crust.

Honey Oatmeal Bread

Pour water into a 3 to 4 qt glass mixing bowl.

> 16 oz cool Water

Add salt, yeast and honey… give a quick stir to combine.

> 1-1/2 tsp Salt
> 1/4 tsp Instant Yeast
> 1 Tbsp Honey

Add flour… then oats (if oats are added before flour they will absorb the water and it will be harder to combine)… stir until dough forms a shaggy ball, scrape dry flour from side of bowl, then tumble dough to combine moist flour with dry flour.

> 3-1/2 cups Bread Flour
> 1 cup Old Fashioned Quaker Oats

Cover bowl with plastic wrap, place on counter, and proof for 8 to 24 hours.

8 to 24 hours later (PMDO | garnish | toaster oven)

When dough has risen and developed its gluten structure… spray bread pan (8-1/2" x 4-1/2" or 9" x 5") with no-stick cooking spray and set aside.

"Degas, pull and stretch"… stick handle end of a plastic spoon in the dough and stir (dough will form a sticky ball). Then, scrape side of bowl to get remainder of the dough into the sticky dough ball.

Garnish… sprinkle dough ball and side of bowl with oats, and roll-to-coat (roll dough ball in oats to coat).

> 1/4 cup Old Fashioned Quaker Oats

Roll dough out of bowl into bread pan.

Cover bottom pan with top pan, secure with binder clips, and place PMDO in a warm draft-free location to proof for 30 minutes.

30 minutes later

Place PMDO in toaster oven, set oven to 400 degrees F, and bake for 45 minutes with the top on and 3 to 10 with the top off to finish the crust.

45 to 55 minutes later

Remove pan from oven, gently turn loaf out on work surface and place on cooling rack.

Honey Whole Wheat Bread (PMDO)

This whole wheat recipe balances the nutrition and nutty taste of whole wheat with the crumb of a Country White in a hearty, moist loaf with a touch of honey for sweetness.

Picture: For lunch I made two deli-fresh sandwiches... one turkey and one ham. I spread mayo on two slices fresh-from-the-oven honey whole wheat bread, added several slices of meat, then topped them with lettuce, tomato, and cheese.

Options:
"Turbo" method: If you wish to reduce the proofing time from 8 hours to 1-1/2 hours... increase yeast from 1/4 to 1-1/4 tsp and proof in a warm draft free environment (78 to 85 degrees F).
Conventional oven: Preheat oven to 400 degrees F. and bake for 40 minutes with the top on and 3 to 15 minutes with the top off to finish the crust.

Honey Whole Wheat Bread

Pour water into a 3 to 4 qt glass mixing bowl.

> 16 oz cool Water

Add salt, yeast, olive oil and honey... give a quick stir to combine.

> 1-1/2 tsp Salt
> 1/4 tsp Instant Yeast
> 1 Tbsp extra-virgin Olive Oil
> 1 Tbsp Honey

Add flour... stir until dough forms a shaggy ball, scrape dry flour from side of bowl, then tumble dough to combine moist flour with dry flour.

> 1-1/2 cups Bread Flour
> 2 cups Whole Wheat Flour

Cover bowl with plastic wrap, place on counter, and proof for 8 to 24 hours.

8 to 24 hours later (PMDO | toaster oven)

When dough has risen and developed its gluten structure... spray bread pan (8-1/2" x 4-1/2" or 9" x 5") with no-stick cooking spray and set aside.

"Degas, pull and stretch"... stick handle end of a plastic spoon in the dough and stir (dough will form a sticky ball). Then, scrape side of bowl to get remainder of the dough into the sticky dough ball.

Roll dough out of bowl into bread pan.

Cover bottom pan with top pan, secure with binder clips, and place PMDO in a warm draft-free location to proof for 30 minutes.

30 minutes later

Place PMDO in toaster oven, set oven to 400 degrees F, and bake for 45 minutes with the top on and 3 to 10 with the top off to finish the crust.

45 to 55 minutes later

Remove pan from oven, gently turn loaf out on work surface and place on cooling rack.

Harvest 8 Grain Whole Wheat Bread (PMDO)

This Harvest 8 Grain Wheat Bread has a more robust and complex flavor than the multigrain country white and wheat breads. I experimented with and tested a number of my own multigrain mixtures before discovering King Arthur's Harvest Grains Blend and (as they state on their website) the whole oat berries, millet, rye flakes and wheat flakes enhance texture while the flax, poppy, sesame, and sunflower seeds add crunch and great, nutty flavor. Wow, the flavor is great... and it's a lot easier and... more practical... to purchase a blend of seeds. You should experiment with blends available in your community.

Because whole wheat loaves can be a little too heavy and dense for some tastes... I like to balance the nutritional value of whole wheat with the crumb and texture of bread flour by using a blend.

Picture: For lunch I made a roast beef & bacon sandwich. I spread mayo on two slices fresh-from-the-oven harvest 8 grain whole wheat bread, added lettuce, sliced roast beef, and a couple slices of bacon.

Options:
"Turbo" method: If you wish to reduce the proofing time from 8 hours to 1-1/2 hours... increase yeast from 1/4 to 1-1/4 tsp and proof in a warm draft free environment (78 to 85 degrees F).
Conventional oven: Preheat oven to 400 degrees F. and bake for 40 minutes with the top on and 3 to 15 minutes with the top off to finish the crust.

Harvest 8 Grain Whole Wheat Bread

Pour water into a 3 to 4 qt glass mixing bowl.

> 18 oz cool Water

Add salt, yeast, olive oil and grains... give a quick stir to combine.

> 1-1/2 tsp Salt
> 1/4 tsp Instant Yeast
> 1 Tbsp extra-virgin Olive Oil
> 2/3 cup King Arthur Harvest Grains Blend

Add flour... stir until dough forms a shaggy ball, scrape dry flour from side of bowl, then tumble dough to combine moist flour with dry flour.

> 1-1/2 cups Bread Flour
> 2 cups Whole Wheat Flour

Cover bowl with plastic wrap, place on counter, and proof for 8 to 24 hours.

8 to 24 hours later (PMDO | garnish & baste | toaster oven)

When dough has risen and developed its gluten structure... spray bread pan (8-1/2" x 4-1/2" or 9" x 5") with no-stick cooking spray and set aside.

"Degas, pull and stretch"... stick handle end of a plastic spoon in the dough and stir (dough will form a sticky ball). Then, scrape side of bowl to get remainder of the dough into the sticky dough ball.

Garnish... sprinkle dough ball and side of bowl with grains, and roll-to-coat (roll dough ball in grains to coat).

> 2 Tbsp King Arthur Harvest Grains Blend

Baste (optional)... place 1 egg yolk in a small mixing bowl, add water, and whip with a fork to combine. Then pour egg wash into mixing bowl and roll-to-coat.

> 1 lg Egg Yolk
> 1 tsp Water

Roll dough out of bowl into bread pan.

Cover bottom pan with top pan, secure with binder clips, and place PMDO in a warm draft-free location to proof for 30 minutes.

30 minutes later

Place PMDO in toaster oven, set oven to 400 degrees F, and bake for 45 minutes with the top on and 3 to 10 with the top off to finish the crust.

45 to 55 minutes later

Remove pan from oven, gently turn loaf out on work surface and place on cooling rack.

Deli Rye Bread (PMDO)
This is a rustic deli rye bread, with a mild rye flavor and a generous amount of caraway seeds that would be the perfect complement to a pastrami sandwich.

Picture: For lunch I made a simple pastrami sandwich. I spread mayo and yellow mustard on two slices fresh-from-the-oven deli rye bread and added 5 slices of pastrami.

YouTube Video in support of recipe: World's Easiest No-Knead Deli Rye Bread (no mixer... "hands-free" technique)

Options:
"Turbo" method: If you wish to reduce the proofing time from 8 hours to 1-1/2 hours... increase yeast from 1/4 to 1-1/4 tsp and proof in a warm draft free environment (78 to 85 degrees F).
Conventional oven: Preheat oven to 400 degrees F. and bake for 40 minutes with the top on and 3 to 15 minutes with the top off to finish the crust.

Deli Rye Bread

Pour water into a 3 to 4 qt glass mixing bowl.

> 14 oz cool Water

Add salt, yeast, sugar, olive oil and seeds... give a quick stir to combine.

> 1-1/2 tsp Salt
> 1/2 tsp Instant Yeast
> 1 Tbsp Sugar
> 2 Tbsp Caraway Seeds
> 1 Tbsp extra-virgin Olive Oil

Add flour... stir until dough forms a shaggy ball, scrape dry flour from side of bowl, then tumble dough to combine moist flour with dry flour.

> 2-1/2 cups Bread Flour
> 1 cup Rye Flour

Cover bowl with plastic wrap, place on counter, and proof for 8 to 24 hours.

8 to 24 hours later (PMDO | toaster oven)

When dough has risen and developed its gluten structure... spray bread pan (8-1/2" x 4-1/2" or 9" x 5") with no-stick cooking spray and set aside.

"Degas, pull and stretch"... stick handle end of a plastic spoon in the dough and stir (dough will form a sticky ball). Then, scrape side of bowl to get remainder of the dough into the sticky dough ball.

Roll dough out of bowl into bread pan.

Cover bottom pan with top pan, secure with binder clips, and place PMDO in a warm draft-free location to proof for 30 minutes.

30 minutes later

Place PMDO in toaster oven, set oven to 400 degrees F, and bake for 45 minutes with the top on and 3 to 10 with the top off to finish the crust.

45 to 55 minutes later

Remove pan from oven, gently turn loaf out on work surface and place on cooling rack.

Buttermilk Bread (small PMDO)

If you like buttermilk ranch dressing… you'll like buttermilk bread. And this isn't the average buttermilk bread… this is an artisan loaf with an airy crumb and tender crust. The appearance is excellent… the taste is great. Buttermilk is a great all-purpose bread. Buttermilk gives it a rich tangy flavor with a subtle buttery depth that is great for sandwiches and toast. I used two undersized *Wilton* 8-1/2" x 4-1/2" bread pans for my PMDO.

It is a common misconception to associate buttermilk with the richness of butter because buttermilk does not have butterfat. Buttermilk is the liquid remaining after taking the butter fat out of the milk in the process of making butter, thus it is lower in calories and fat than butter and higher in calcium, vitamin B12 and potassium than regular milk. And it's important to use cultured buttermilk, if you substitute 2% for cultured buttermilk in this recipe it will upset the balance of wet and dry ingredients (it's thinner), and you don't want to lose the nutritional value of buttermilk. After all, you wouldn't want to take the "yo" out of yogurt.

Note: The recipe uses 1 tsp (versus 1/4) instant yeast because dairy products, like buttermilk, retard yeast activity.

Picture: For lunch I made a deli-fresh turkey sandwich. I spread mayo on two slices fresh-from-the-oven buttermilk bread, added deli-fresh turkey, lettuce and a slice of tomato.

Buttermilk Bread

Pour buttermilk and water to a 3 to 4 qt glass mixing bowl.

> 8 oz Cultured Buttermilk
>
> 6 oz cool Water

Add salt, yeast, sugar and oil... give a quick stir to combine.

> 1-1/2 tsp Salt
>
> 1 tsp Instant Yeast
>
> 1 Tbsp Sugar
>
> 1 Tbsp Vegetable Oil

Add flour... stir until dough forms a shaggy ball, scrape dry flour from side of bowl, then tumble dough to combine moist flour with dry flour.

> 3 cups Bread Flour

Cover bowl with plastic wrap, place on counter, and proof for 8 to 24 hours.

8 to 24 hours later (small PMDO | garnish | toaster oven)

When dough has risen and developed its gluten structure... spray bread pan (8" x 4") with no-stick cooking spray and set aside.

"Degas, pull and stretch"... stick handle end of a plastic spoon in the dough and stir (dough will form a sticky ball). Then, scrape side of bowl to get remainder of the dough into the sticky dough ball.

Garnish... sprinkle dough ball and side of bowl with sesame seeds, and roll-to-coat (roll dough ball in seeds to coat).

> 2 Tbsp Sesame Seeds

Roll dough out of bowl into bread pan.

Cover bottom pan with top pan, secure with binder clips, and place PMDO in a warm draft-free location to proof for 30 minutes.

30 minutes later

Place PMDO in toaster oven, set oven to 400 degrees F, and bake for 40 minutes with the top on and 3 to 10 with the top off to finish the crust.

40 to 50 minutes later

Remove pan from oven, gently turn loaf out on work surface and place on cooling rack.

Cinnamon Raisin Bread (small PMDO)

Homemade fresh-from-the-oven cinnamon raisin bread is a great way to start your day and when our guests stay overnight, my wife wants them to wake up to the aroma of fresh for the oven cinnamon raisin bread filling the house. I used two *Good Cook* 8" x 4" bread pans for my PMDO. Raisin bread is ideally suited for a smaller bread pan.

Note: This recipe has several variations... (a) I used 1 tsp (vs 1/4 tsp) instant yeast because cinnamon retards yeast activity. (b) I increased the baking time with the top on by 10 minutes (50 vs 40 for small bread pans) because the raisins added mass and moisture. And (c) I did not bake it with the top off because cinnamon raisin bread is naturally brown in color and doesn't need the extra baking time to finish the crust.

Option:
"Turbo" method: If you wish to reduce the proofing time from 8 hours to 1-1/2 to 2 hours... increase yeast from 1 to 2-1/4 tsp yeast and proof in a warm draft free environment (78 to 85 degrees F).
Conventional oven: Preheat oven to 400 degrees F. and bake for 40 minutes with the top on and 3 to 5 minutes with the top off to finish the crust.

Cinnamon Raisin Bread

Pour water into a 3 to 4 qt glass mixing bowl.

> 14 oz cool Water

Add salt, yeast, sugar and cinnamon... give a quick stir to combine with a flat whisk or fork (it will make it easier to combine the cinnamon).

> 1-1/2 tsp Salt
> 1 tsp Instant Yeast
> 2 Tbsp Brown Sugar
> 1 Tbsp ground Cinnamon

Add flour... then raisins. Stir until dough forms a shaggy ball, scrape dry flour from side of bowl, then tumble dough to combine moist flour with dry flour.

> 3 cups Bread Flour
> 1 cup Raisins

Cover bowl with plastic wrap, place on counter, and proof for 8 to 24 hours.

8 to 24 hours later (small PMDO | toaster oven)

When dough has risen and developed its gluten structure... spray bread pan (8" x 4") with no-stick cooking spray and set aside.

"Degas, pull and stretch"... stick handle end of a plastic spoon in the dough and stir (dough will form a sticky ball). Then, scrape side of bowl to get remainder of the dough into the sticky dough ball.

Roll dough out of bowl into bread pan.

Cover bottom pan with top pan, secure with binder clips, and place PMDO in a warm draft-free location to proof for 30 minutes.

30 minutes later

Place PMDO in toaster oven, set oven to 400 degrees F, and bake for 50 minutes (typically I would bake a standard 3 cup loaf in a 4" x 8" bread pan for 40 minutes, but raisin bread may need to be baked for an additional 5 to 10 minutes because of the moisture and density of the raisins).

50 minutes later

Remove PMDO from oven, gently turn loaf out on work surface and place on cooling rack.

Garlic Bread (long PMDO)

All of us like garlic cheese bread... I like to lightly infuse the garlic into the loaf. It gives the loaf a nice full flavor and it's easier than adding garlic after the fact. I used two *Wilton* 12" x 4-1/2" long bread pans for my PMDO.

Picture: As an appetizer for dinner I served garlic cheese bread. Because the garlic is already infused in the bread, all I needed to do was... toast two slices, spread on a little butter, add a little cheese, a sprinkle of salt, and broil them in the toaster oven to melt the cheese.

Options:

Half-loaves: Use two sets of long loaf pans (12" x 4-1/2"), dust with flour (roll-to-coat), divide dough in half, shape, and bake at 400 degrees for 35 minutes with the top on and 3 to 5 with the top off.

"Turbo" method: If you wish to reduce the proofing time from 8 hours to 1-1/2 hours... increase yeast from 1/4 to 1-1/4 tsp and proof in a warm draft free environment (78 to 85 degrees F).

Conventional oven: Preheat oven to 400 degrees F. and bake for 35 minutes with the top on and 3 to 15 minutes with the top off to finish the crust.

Garlic Bread

Pour water into a 3 to 4 qt glass mixing bowl.

> 14 oz cool Water

Add salt, yeast, garlic and olive oil... give a quick stir to combine.

> 1-1/2 tsp Salt
> 1/4 tsp Instant Yeast
> 1 heaping tsp Minced Garlic (jar)
> 1 Tbsp extra-virgin Olive Oil

Add flour... stir until dough forms a shaggy ball, scrape dry flour from side of bowl, then tumble dough to combine moist flour with dry flour.

> 3-1/2 cups Bread Flour

Cover bowl with plastic wrap, place on counter, and proof for 8 to 24 hours.

8 to 24 hours later (long PMDO | dust with flour | toaster oven)

When dough has risen and developed its gluten structure... spray long bread pan (12" x 4-1/2") with no-stick cooking spray and set aside.

"Degas, pull and stretch"... stick handle end of a plastic spoon in the dough and stir (dough will form a sticky ball). Then, scrape side of bowl to get remainder of the dough into the sticky dough ball.

"Roll-to-coat"... sprinkle dough ball and side of bowl with flour and roll-to-coat (dusting dough ball with flour will make it easier to handle and shape the dough for the baker).

> 2 Tbsp Bread Flour

Dust work surface with flour, roll dough (and excess flour) out of bowl onto work surface, roll dough on work surface in flour to shape, and place in long bread pan.

Cover bottom pan with top pan, secure with binder clips, and place PMDO in a warm draft-free location to proof for 30 minutes.

30 minutes later

Place PMDO in toaster oven, set oven to 400 degrees F, and bake for 40 minutes with the top on and 3 to 10 with the top off to finish the crust.

40 to 50 minutes later

Remove pan from oven, gently turn loaf out on work surface and place on cooling rack.

Mediterranean Olive Bread (long covered baker)

If a restaurant served you this loaf as their signature bread... you'd be talking about it for years and you'd be surprised how easy it is to make. I slice the green and Kalamata olives in half and increased the baking time with the top on by 5 minutes (45 vs. 40 long PMDO) because olives added mass and moisture.

Options:

<u>"Traditional" method</u>: If you wish to proof overnight using the traditional method... decrease yeast from 1-1/4 tsp to 1/4 tsp and proof 8 to 24 hours.

<u>Conventional oven</u>: Preheat oven to 400 degrees F. and bake for 40 minutes with the top on and 3 to 15 minutes with the top off to finish the crust.

Mediterranean Olive Bread

Prepare flavor ingredients... zest lemon, open black olives, slice green olives and kalamata olives in half, and set flavor ingredients aside.

> Zest of 1 Lemon
> 1/4 cup (2-1/4 oz can) sliced Black Olives
> 1/4 cup stuffed Green Olives (use black olive can to measure)
> 1/4 cup pitted Kalamata Olives (use black olive can to measure)

Pour water into a 3 to 4 qt glass mixing bowl.

> 14 oz cool Water

Add salt, yeast, thyme and olive oil... give a quick stir to combine.

> 1-1/2 tsp Salt
> 1-1/4 tsp Instant Yeast
> 1 tsp dried Thyme
> 1 Tbsp extra-virgin Olive Oil

Add flour... then flavor ingredients. Stir until dough forms a shaggy ball, scrape dry flour from side of bowl, then tumble dough to combine moist flour with dry flour.

> 3-1/2 cups Bread Flour
> Flavor ingredients (above)

Cover bowl with plastic wrap, place in a warm draft-free location, and proof for 1-1/2 hours.

1-1/2 hours later (long covered baker | dust with flour | toaster oven)

When dough has risen and developed its gluten structure... spray bottom portion of a long covered baker (12" x 4-1/2") with no-stick cooking spray and set aside.

"Degas, pull and stretch"... stick handle end of a plastic spoon in the dough and stir (dough will form a sticky ball). Then, scrape side of bowl to get remainder of the dough into the sticky dough ball.

"Roll-to-coat"... sprinkle dough ball and side of bowl with flour and roll-to-coat (dusting dough ball with flour will make it easier to handle and shape the dough for the baker).

> 2 Tbsp Bread Flour

Dust work surface with flour, roll dough (and excess flour) out of bowl onto work surface, roll dough on work surface in flour to shape, and place in baker.

Cover baker with top and place in a warm draft-free location to proof for 30 minutes.

30 minutes later

Place long covered baker in toaster oven, set oven to 400 degrees F, and bake for 45 minutes with the top on and 3 to 10 with the top off to finish the crust.

45 to 55 minutes later

Remove from oven, gently turn loaves out on work surface and place on cooling rack.

Long Half Loaves (2 long PMDO)
Half loaves are excellent for demi sandwiches and crostini. I used 4 *Wilton* long loaf pan (12" x 4-1/2") for my PMDOs.

Options:
<u>"Traditional" method</u>: If you wish to proof overnight using the traditional method... decrease yeast from 1-1/4 tsp to 1/4 tsp and proof 8 to 24 hours.
<u>Conventional oven</u>: Preheat oven to 400 degrees F. and bake for 25 minutes with the top on and 3 to 15 minutes with the top off to finish the crust.

Long Half Loaves

Pour warm water in a 3 to 4 qt warm glass mixing bowl (use a warm bowl... you don't want a cold bowl to take the heat out of the warm water).

> 14 oz warm Water

Add salt and yeast... give a quick stir to combine.

> 1-1/2 tsp Salt
> 1-1/4 tsp Instant Yeast

Add flour... stir until dough forms a shaggy ball, scrape dry flour from side of bowl, then tumble dough to combine moist flour with dry flour.

> 3-1/2 cups Bread Flour

Cover bowl with plastic wrap, place in a warm draft-free location, and proof for 1-1/2 hours.

1-1/2 hours later (long loaf pans | toaster oven)

When dough has risen and developed its gluten structure... spray 2 long loaf pans (12" x 4-1/2") with no-stick cooking spray, and set aside.

"Degas, pull and stretch"... stick handle end of a plastic spoon in the dough and stir (dough will form a sticky ball). Then, scrape side of bowl to get remainder of the dough into the sticky dough ball.

"Roll-to-coat"... sprinkle dough ball and side of bowl with flour and roll-to-coat (dusting dough ball with flour will make it easier to handle and shape dough).

> 2 Tbsp Bread Flour

Dust work surface with flour, roll dough (and excess flour) out of bowl onto work surface.

Press lightly to flatten and divide dough into 2 portions, then (one portion at a time)... roll dough on work surface in flour to shape (adding flour as needed) and place in pan (pan will finish shaping loaf for you).

Cover bottom pan with top pan, secure with binder clips, and place PMDO in a warm draft-free location to proof for 30 minutes.

30 minutes later

Place PMDOs in toaster oven side-by-side, set oven to 400 degrees F, and bake for 30 minutes with the top on and 3 to 10 minutes with the top off to finish the crust.

30 to 40 minutes later

Remove from oven, gently turn loaves out on work surface and place on cooling rack.

Rosemary Appetizer Loaves (3 small PMDO)

I was so thrilled with the appetizer loaves at *Macaroni Grill* that I decided to make my own and developed a rosemary appetizer demi loaf recipe that required kneading. Then my wife found a no-knead ciabatta bread recipe in the local newspaper... I was converted. I experimented with no-knead recipes and converted my old rosemary appetizer loaf recipe to the no-knead method. That was the beginning and I haven't looked back. I use 6 *Good Cook* bread pans (8" x 4") to shape the loaves.

Options:

Traditional method: If you wish to proof overnight... use cool Water, 1/4 tsp instant Yeast, and proof 8 to 24 hours.

Conventional oven: Preheat oven to 400 degrees F. and bake for 30 minutes with the top on and 3 to 15 minutes with the top off to finish the crust.

Rosemary Appetizer Loaves

Pour warm water in a 3 to 4 qt warm glass mixing bowl (use a warm bowl... you don't want a cold bowl to take the heat out of the warm water).

14 oz warm Water

Add salt, yeast, rosemary and olive oil... give a quick stir to combine.

1-1/2 tsp Salt

1-1/4 tsp Instant Yeast

1 Tbsp dried Rosemary

1 Tbsp extra-virgin Olive Oil

Add flour... stir until dough forms a shaggy ball, scrape dry flour from side of bowl, then tumble dough to combine moist flour with dry flour.

3-1/2 cups Bread Flour

Cover bowl with plastic wrap, place in a warm draft-free location, and proof for 1-1/2 hours.

1-1/2 hours later (3 small PMDO | toaster oven)

When dough has risen and developed its gluten structure... spray 3 small bread pans (8" x 4") with no-stick cooking spray and set aside.

"Degas, pull and stretch"... stick handle end of a plastic spoon in the dough and stir (dough will form a sticky ball). Then, scrape side of bowl to get remainder of the dough into the sticky dough ball.

"Roll-to-coat"... sprinkle dough ball and side of bowl with flour and roll-to-coat (dusting dough ball with flour will make it easier to handle and shape dough).

2 Tbsp Bread Flour

Dust work surface with flour, roll dough (and excess flour) out of bowl onto work surface.

Press lightly to flatten and divide dough into 3 portions.

Then (one portion at a time)... roll dough on work surface in flour to shape (adding flour as needed) and place in small bread pan.

Cover bottom pan with top pan, secure with binder clips, and place PMDO in a warm draft-free location to proof for 30 minutes.

30 minutes later

Place PMDOs in toaster oven, set oven to 400 degrees F, and bake for 35 minutes with the top on and 3 to 10 minutes with the top off to finish the crust.

35 to 45 minutes later

Remove from oven, gently turn loaves out on work surface and place on cooling rack.

Traditional Dinner Rolls (PMDO jumbo muffin pans)

These dinner rolls are simple and basic. If you're making your first batch of rolls this is the place to start. The rolls don't require any shaping... just "plop" the dough in a jumbo muffin pan and the pan will shape the rolls for you. I used 2 *Wilton* jumbo muffin pans to form a PMDO. Using 2 jumbo muffin pans to form a PMDO will give you a lighter softer crust, but it isn't necessary (see "Options").

Options:

Traditional method: If you wish to proof overnight... use cool Water, 1/4 tsp instant Yeast, and proof 8 to 24 hours.

Non-PMDO: If you only have one jumbo muffin pan... place pan in toaster oven, set oven to 450 degrees F, and bake for 20 minutes.

Conventional oven: Move rack to middle of oven, pre-heat to 450 degrees F. and bake for 20 minutes.

Traditional Dinner Rolls

Pour warm water in a 2-1/2 to 3-1/2 qt warm glass mixing bowl (use a warm bowl... you don't want a cold bowl to take the heat out of the warm water).

> 12 oz warm Water

Add salt and yeast... give a quick stir to combine.

> 1-1/2 tsp Salt
> 1-1/4 tsp Instant Yeast

Add flour... stir until dough forms a shaggy ball, scrape dry flour from side of bowl, then tumble dough to combine moist flour with dry flour.

> 3 cups Bread Flour

Cover bowl with plastic wrap, place in a warm draft-free location, and proof for 1-1/2 hours.

1-1/2 hours later (PMDO using jumbo muffin pans | toaster oven)

When dough has risen and developed its gluten structure... spray bottom jumbo muffin pan with no-stick cooking spray and set the two pans aside.

"Degas, pull and stretch"... stick handle end of a plastic spoon in the dough and stir (dough will form a sticky ball). Then, scrape side of bowl to get remainder of the dough into the sticky dough ball.

"Roll-to-coat"... sprinkle dough ball and side of bowl with flour and roll-to-coat (dusting dough ball with flour will make it easier to handle and shape dough).

> 2 Tbsp Bread Flour

Dust work surface with flour, roll dough (and excess flour) out of bowl onto work surface.

Press lightly to flatten and divide dough into 6 portions (divide into 3 portions then divide each portion in half) and place 1 portion in each cavity (cavity will shape roll for you).

Cover bottom pan with top pan, secure with binder clips, and place PMDO in a warm draft-free location to proof for 30 minutes.

30 minutes later

Place pans in toaster oven, set oven to 400 degrees F, and bake for 20 minutes with the top on and 5 to 10 minutes with the top off to finish the crust.

25 to 30 minutes later

Remove from oven, gently turn rolls out on work surface and place on cooling rack.

Hamburger Buns (PMDO mini round cake pans)

I frequently use store bought hamburger buns, but there are times when I'm looking for something special and a fresh-from-the-oven artisan bun can change a good hamburger into a great dining experience. You'll never find a hamburger bun like these in a grocery store. I used 12 *Wilton* mini round cake pans to form 6 PMDOs to protect the crust and shape the buns.

Options:

<u>Traditional method</u>: If you wish to proof overnight... use cool Water, 1/4 tsp instant Yeast, and proof 8 to 24 hours.

<u>Conventional oven</u>: Move rack to middle of oven, pre-heat to 450 degrees F. and bake for 20 minutes.

Hamburger Buns

Pour warm water in a 2-1/2 to 3-1/2 qt warm glass mixing bowl (use a warm bowl… you don't want a cold bowl to take the heat out of the warm water).

> 12 oz warm Water

Add salt and yeast… give a quick stir to combine.

> 1-1/2 tsp Salt
> 1-1/4 tsp Instant Yeast

Add flour… stir until dough forms a shaggy ball, scrape dry flour from side of bowl, then tumble dough to combine moist flour with dry flour.

> 3 cups Bread Flour

Cover bowl with plastic wrap, place in a warm draft-free location, and proof for 1-1/2 hours.

1-1/2 hours later (PMDO mini round cake pans | toaster oven)

When dough has risen and developed its gluten structure… spray 6 mini round cake pans (4" x 1-1/4") with no-stick cooking spray, place in rimmed baking sheet (makes it easier to carry them), and set aside.

"Degas, pull and stretch"… stick handle end of a plastic spoon in the dough and stir (dough will form a sticky ball). Then, scrape side of bowl to get remainder of the dough into the sticky dough ball.

"Roll-to-coat"… sprinkle dough ball and side of bowl with flour and roll-to-coat (dusting dough ball with flour will make it easier to handle and shape dough).

> 2 Tbsp Bread Flour

Dust work surface with flour, roll dough (and excess flour) out of bowl onto work surface.

Press lightly to flatten and divide dough into 6 portions (divide into 3 portions then divide each portion in half) and place 1 portion in each pan (pan will shape roll for you).

Cover bottom pans with top pans, secure with small binder clips, and place rimmed baking sheet in a warm draft-free location to proof for 30 minutes.

30 minutes later

Place rimmed baking sheet in toaster oven, set oven to 400 degrees F, and bake for 20 minutes with the top on and 5 to 10 minutes with the top off to finish the crust.

25 to 30 minutes later

Remove from oven, gently turn buns out on work surface and place on cooling rack.

Prefect Little 9" No-Knead Pizza

The Perfect Little 9" Pizza was designed to be baked in a toaster oven, but it can also be baked in a conventional oven. It's ideal for individual servings or as an appetizer.

Conventional vs. Toaster Oven
When I bake "Perfect Little 9" Pizzas" in the regular oven, I preheat the oven and bake them at 450 degrees F for 12 to 15 minutes, but my toaster oven heats faster and bakes hotter so I bake them at 400 degrees for 8 to 10 minutes (it isn't necessary to preheat a toaster oven).

Recipes are written to be baked in a conventional oven, but the process, bakeware, and size of the pizza were written and designed for a toaster oven because toaster ovens come in a variety of sizes... and you may need to slightly adapt the baking time and temperature to your toaster oven.

Saving Dough
If you wish to save dough... divide into portions, drizzle each portion with olive oil, place in zip-lock bag, remove excess air, and refrigerate for up to two days or freeze for up to two months. To thaw dough... move dough from freezer to refrigerator the day before (12 or more hours), then place on counter for 30 minutes before use to come to room temperature.

YouTube video in support of recipe: <u>How to Make Homemade Perfect Little 9"</u> <u>Pizza in a Toaster Oven (No-Knead "Turbo" Pizza Dough)</u>

Small Batch "Turbo" Pizza Dough

Pour warm water in a 2-1/2 to 3-1/2 qt warm glass mixing bowl (use a warm bowl... you don't want a cold bowl to take the heat out of the warm water).

> 6 oz warm Water

Add salt, yeast, and olive oil... give a quick stir to combine.

> 1 tsp Salt
>
> 1 tsp Instant Yeast
>
> 2 tsp extra-virgin Olive Oil

Add flour... stir until dough forms a shaggy ball, scrape dry flour from side of bowl, then tumble dough to combine moist flour with dry flour.

> 1-1/2 cups Bread Flour

Cover bowl with plastic wrap, place in a warm draft-free location, and proof for 1-1/2 hours.

1-1/2 hours later

When dough has risen and developed its gluten structure...

"Degas, pull and stretch"... stick handle end of a plastic spoon in the dough and stir (the dough will form a sticky ball). Then, scrape the side of the bowl to get the remainder of the dough into the sticky dough ball.

"Roll-to-coat"... sprinkle dough ball and side of bowl with flour and roll-to-coat (dusting dough ball with flour will make it easier to handle and shape dough).

> 2 Tbsp Bread Flour

Dust work surface with flour, roll dough (and excess flour) out of bowl onto work surface.

Press lightly to flatten... divide dough into 2 portions and form each portion into a ball.

If you aren't ready to use the pizza dough balls... cover with a lint-free towel to rest.

Options:

Mix & Match – You can use small batch pizza dough balls for either 12" pizzas or Perfect Little 9" Pizzas. My wife and I frequently make one of each.

Traditional Method – Decrease yeast from 1 tsp to 1/4 tsp and proof over night.

Large Batch "Turbo" Pizza Dough

Pour warm water in a 2-1/2 to 3-1/2 qt warm glass mixing bowl (use a warm bowl... you don't want a cold bowl to take the heat out of the warm water).

<u>14 oz warm Water</u>

Add salt, yeast, and olive oil... give a quick stir to combine.

<u>1-1/2 tsp Salt</u>
<u>1-1/2 tsp Instant Yeast</u>
<u>1 Tbsp extra-virgin Olive Oil</u>

Add flour... stir until dough forms a shaggy ball, scrape dry flour from side of bowl, then tumble dough to combine moist flour with dry flour.

<u>3-1/2 cups Bread Flour</u>

Cover bowl with plastic wrap, place in a warm draft-free location, and proof for 1-1/2 hours.

1-1/2 hours later

When dough has risen and developed its gluten structure...

"Degas, pull and stretch"... stick handle end of a plastic spoon in the dough and stir (the dough will form a sticky ball). Then, scrape the side of the bowl to get the remainder of the dough into the sticky dough ball.

"Roll-to-coat"... sprinkle dough ball and side of bowl with flour and roll-to-coat (dusting dough ball with flour will make it easier to handle and shape dough).

<u>2 Tbsp Bread Flour</u>

Dust work surface with flour, roll dough (and excess flour) out of bowl onto work surface.

Press lightly to flatten... divide dough into 2 portions and form each portion into a ball.

If you aren't ready to use the pizza dough balls... cover with a lint-free towel to rest.

Options:

<u>Mix & Match</u> – You can use small batch pizza dough balls for either 12" pizzas or Perfect Little 9" Pizzas. My wife and I frequently make one of each.

<u>Traditional Method</u> – Decrease yeast from 1 tsp to 1/4 tsp and proof over night.

Small Batch "Turbo" Whole Wheat Pizza Dough

Pour warm water in a 2-1/2 to 3-1/2 qt warm glass mixing bowl (use a warm bowl... you don't want a cold bowl to take the heat out of the warm water).

   6 oz warm Water

Add salt, yeast, and olive oil... give a quick stir to combine.

   1 tsp Salt
   1 tsp Instant Yeast
   2 tsp extra-virgin Olive Oil
   1 tsp Honey (option)

Add flour... stir until dough forms a shaggy ball, scrape dry flour from side of bowl, then tumble dough to combine moist flour with dry flour.

   3/4 cup Bread Flour
   3/4 cup Whole Wheat Flour

Cover bowl with plastic wrap, place in a warm draft-free location, and proof for 1-1/2 hours.

1-1/2 hours later

When dough has risen and developed its gluten structure...

"Degas, pull and stretch"... stick handle end of a plastic spoon in the dough and stir (the dough will form a sticky ball). Then, scrape the side of the bowl to get the remainder of the dough into the sticky dough ball.

"Roll-to-coat"... sprinkle dough ball and side of bowl with flour and roll-to-coat (dusting dough ball with flour will make it easier to handle and shape dough).

   2 Tbsp Bread Flour

Dust work surface with flour, roll dough (and excess flour) out of bowl onto work surface.

Press lightly to flatten... divide dough into 2 portions and form each portion into a ball.

If you aren't ready to use the pizza dough balls... cover with a lint-free towel to rest.

Options:

100% Whole Wheat – You can use 1-1/2 cups Whole Wheat Flour.

Mix & Match – You can use small batch pizza dough balls for either 12" pizzas or Perfect Little 9" Pizzas. My wife and I frequently make one of each.

Traditional Method – Decrease yeast from 1 tsp to 1/4 tsp and proof over night.

Perfect Little 9" Pepperoni Pizza

Prep: Move rack to the middle of oven and preheat to 450 degrees F, drizzle 9" pie pan with olive oil and set aside.

       <u>1 tsp extra-virgin Olive Oil</u>

Shape: Generously dust work surface with flour, place dough ball on work space and roll in flour to coat... then press firmly with the palm of your hand to flatten, use pizza roller to shape into a 9" circle and place in pan.

       <u>1 small batch pizza Dough Ball</u>

Finish shaping by pressing dough to cover bottom of pan.

Toppings: Spread a thin layer of sauce (too much sauce will make your crust soggy) on dough, generously sprinkle with cheese, and add pepperoni to cover.

       <u>1 heaping Tbsp Pizza Sauce</u>
       <u>4 oz shredded Provolone-Mozzarella Cheese</u>
       <u>Pepperoni slices</u>

Bake: Put pizza in oven and bake for 12 to 15 minutes depending on the thickness of the crust, the toppings, and how you like your cheese (I like it when the cheese just starts to turn dark brown).

Serve: Remove from oven, slice and serve.

Perfect Little 9" Cheese Pizza

Prep: Move rack to the middle of oven and preheat to 450 degrees F, drizzle 9" pie pan with olive oil and set aside.

    1 tsp extra-virgin Olive Oil

Shape: Generously dust work surface with flour, place dough ball on work space and roll in flour to coat... then press firmly with the palm of your hand to flatten, use pizza roller to shape into a 9" circle and place in pan.

    1 small batch pizza Dough Ball

Finish shaping by pressing dough to cover bottom of pan.

Toppings: Spread a thin layer of sauce on dough and generously cover with cheese.

    1 heaping Tbsp Pizza Sauce

    4 oz shredded Provolone-Mozzarella Cheese

Bake: Put pizza in oven and bake for 12 to 15 minutes depending on the thickness of the crust, the toppings, and how you like your cheese.

Serve: Remove from oven, slice and serve.

Perfect Little 9" Meatball Pizza

Prep: Move rack to the middle of oven and preheat to 450 degrees F, drizzle 9" pie pan with olive oil and set aside.

      1 tsp extra-virgin Olive Oil

Meatballs... place meatballs on a paper plate, microwave on high for 1 minute, cut in half and set aside.

      6 sm frozen Meatballs

Shape: Generously dust work surface with flour, place dough ball on work space and roll in flour to coat... then press firmly with the palm of your hand to flatten, use pizza roller to shape into a 9" circle and place in pan.

      1 small batch pizza Dough Ball

Finish shaping by pressing dough to cover bottom of pan.

Toppings: Spread a thin layer of sauce on dough, generously sprinkle with cheese, add meatballs, and sprinkle with a little more cheese.

      1 heaping Tbsp Pizza Sauce

      4 oz shredded Provolone-Mozzarella Cheese

Bake: Put pizza in oven and bake for 12 to 15 minutes depending on the thickness of the crust, the toppings, and how you like your cheese.

Serve: Remove from oven, slice and serve.

Perfect Little 9" Mushroom-Black Olive Pizza

Prep: Move rack to the middle of oven and preheat to 450 degrees F, drizzle 9" pie pan with olive oil and set aside.

> 1 tsp extra-virgin Olive Oil

Shape: Generously dust work surface with flour, place dough ball on work space and roll in flour to coat... then press firmly with the palm of your hand to flatten, use pizza roller to shape into a 9" circle and place in pan.

> 1 small batch pizza Dough Ball

Finish shaping by pressing dough to cover bottom of pan.

Toppings: Spread a thin layer of sauce on dough, generously sprinkle with cheese, add mushrooms to cover, add black olives, and sprinkle with a little more cheese.

> 1 heaping Tbsp Pizza Sauce
> 4 oz shredded Provolone-Mozzarella Cheese
> Mushrooms
> Sliced Black Olives

Bake: Put pizza in oven and bake for 12 to 15 minutes depending on the thickness of the crust, the toppings, and how you like your cheese.

Serve: Remove from oven, slice and serve.

Perfect Little 9" Veggie Pizza

Prep: Move rack to the middle of oven and preheat to 450 degrees F, drizzle 9" pie pan with olive oil and set aside.

      1 tsp extra-virgin Olive Oil

Shape: Generously dust work surface with flour, place dough ball on work space and roll in flour to coat... then press firmly with the palm of your hand to flatten, use pizza roller to shape into a 9" circle and place in pan.

      1 small batch pizza Dough Ball

Finish shaping by pressing dough to cover bottom of pan.

Toppings: Spread a thin layer of sauce on dough, generously sprinkle with cheese, add vegetables, black olives, and tomato slices, and sprinkle with a little more cheese.

      1 heaping Tbsp Pizza Sauce
      3 oz shredded Provolone-Mozzarella Cheese
      Vegetable Stir-Fry (prepackaged mix of vegetables)
      3 slices Roma Tomato

Bake: Put pizza in oven and bake for 12 to 15 minutes depending on the thickness of the crust, the toppings, and how you like your cheese.

Serve: Remove from oven, slice and serve.

Perfect Little 9" Bacon, Bacon, Bacon Pizza

Prep: Move rack to the middle of oven and preheat to 450 degrees F, drizzle 9" pie pan with olive oil and set aside.

>1 tsp extra-virgin Olive Oil

Canadian bacon… cut into quarters and strips… and set aside.

>2 slices Canadian Bacon

Pre-cooked bacon… cut into 1/2" sections… and set aside.

>2 strips pre-cooked Bacon

Shape: Generously dust work surface with flour, place dough ball on work space and roll in flour to coat… then press firmly with the palm of your hand to flatten, use pizza roller to shape into a 9" circle and place in pan.

>1 small batch pizza Dough Ball

Finish shaping by pressing dough to cover bottom of pan.

Toppings: Spread a thin layer of sauce on dough, generously sprinkle with cheese, cover with Canadian and precooked bacon, then sprinkle with bacon bits and a little more cheese.

>1 heaping Tbsp Pizza Sauce
>4 oz shredded Provolone-Mozzarella Cheese
>2 tsp real Bacon Bits

Bake: Put pizza in oven and bake for 12 to 15 minutes depending on the thickness of the crust, the toppings, and how you like your cheese.

Serve: Remove from oven, slice and serve.

Perfect Little 9" Mexican Jalapeño-Chili Fiesta Pizza

Prep: Move rack to the middle of oven and preheat to 450 degrees F, drizzle 9" pie pan with olive oil and set aside.

    1 tsp extra-virgin Olive Oil

Shape: Generously dust work surface with flour, place dough ball on work space and roll in flour to coat... then press firmly with the palm of your hand to flatten, use pizza roller to shape into a 9" circle and place in pan.

    1 small batch pizza Dough Ball

Finish shaping by pressing dough to cover bottom of pan.

Toppings: Sprinkle with cheese, add chilies, peppers, and corn.

    4 oz shredded Pepper Jack or Provolone-Mozzarella Cheese
    1 whole Green Chilies (sliced lengthwise)
    12 to 16 fresh Jalapeño Peppers slices
    1/4 cup Golden Sweet Corn

Bake: Put pizza in oven and bake for 12 to 15 minutes depending on the thickness of the crust, the toppings, and how you like your cheese.

Serve: Remove from oven, slice and serve.

Perfect Little 9" Cinnamon-Sugar Pizza

Prep: Move rack to the middle of oven and preheat to 450 degrees F, drizzle 9" pie pan with olive oil and set aside.

    1 tsp extra-virgin Olive Oil

Cinnamon-sugar mixture: Put sugar in bowl, add cinnamon, stir to combine, and set aside.

    1 Tbsp White Sugar
    1/2 tsp Cinnamon

Icing: Put powder sugar in medium size bowl, add 2 Tbsp milk, and use a small spatula to combine.

    2 cups Powder Sugar
    3 to 4 Tbsp Whole Milk

Stir until glaze begins to come together, then add 1 more Tbsp milk and continue to stir (it should be close to the correct consistency).

Continue adding milk in very small portions until glaze is thin enough to spread, but not runny. (If the glaze sits a little too long and thickens... add a little more milk and stir to thin.)

Shape: Generously dust work surface with flour, place dough ball on work space and roll in flour to coat... then press firmly with the palm of your hand to flatten, use pizza roller to shape into a 9" circle and place in pan.

    1 small batch pizza Dough Ball

Finish shaping by pressing dough to cover bottom of pan.

Toppings: Brush dough with butter and generously sprinkle with cinnamon-sugar mixture.

    1 Tbsp melted Butter

Bake: Put pizza in oven and bake for 12 minutes.

Serve: Remove from oven, slice, drizzle with icing, and serve.

12" Pizza
You can also shape the Perfect Little 9" Pizza into a 12" pizza.

Prep: Move rack to the middle of oven and preheat to 450 degrees F, drizzle 9" pie pan with olive oil and set aside.

>   1 tsp extra-virgin Olive Oil

Shape: Generously dust work surface with flour, place dough ball on work space and roll in flour to coat... then press firmly with the palm of your hand to flatten, use pizza roller to shape into a 12" circle and place on a 12' pizza pan.

>   1 small batch pizza Dough Ball

Finish shaping by pressing dough to cover pan.

Toppings: Increase the toppings 50% using any of the previous recipes.

Bake: Put pizza in oven and bake for 12 to 15 minutes depending on the thickness of the crust, the toppings, and how you like your cheese.

Serve: Remove from oven, slice and serve.

Made in the USA
Middletown, DE
24 February 2020

85258883R00040